MathStart®
READING A SCHEDULE

Rodeo Time

by Stuart J. Murphy

illustrated by David T. Wenzel

LEVEL 3

HarperCollins*Publishers*

To Camille Sophia,
who arrived right on schedule—
our third wonderful grandchild
—S.J.M.

To my sister Lisa.
You and Reveille are still providing
inspiration for my equestrian sketches
—D.W.

The publisher and author would like to thank teachers Patricia Chase, Phyllis Goldman, and Patrick Hopfensperger for their help in making the math in MathStart just right for kids.

HarperCollins®, ®, and MathStart® are registered trademarks of HarperCollins Publishers.
For more information about the MathStart series, write to
HarperCollins Children's Books, 1350 Avenue of the Americas, New York, NY 10019,
or visit our website at www.mathstartbooks.com.

Bugs incorporated in the MathStart series design were painted by Jon Buller.

Rodeo Time

Manufactured in China by South China Printing Company Ltd.

Library of Congress Cataloging-in-Publication Data
Murphy, Stuart J.
Rodeo time / by Stuart J. Murphy ; illustrated by David T. Wenzel.— 1st ed.
p. cm. — (MathStart)
"Level 3."
ISBN-10: 0-06-055779-6 (pbk.) — ISBN-10: 0-06-055778-8
ISBN-13: 978-0-06-055779-9 (pbk.) — ISBN-13: 978-0-06-055778-2
1. Time—Juvenile literature. 2. Rodeos—Juvenile literature. I. Wenzel, David, 1950- ill. II. Title. III. Series.
QB209.5.M89 2006 2005002665
529'.7—dc22 CIP
AC

Typography by Elynn Cohen 1 2 3 4 5 6 7 8 9 10 ❖ First Edition

Be sure to look for all of these **MathStart** books:

LEVEL 1

Beep Beep, Vroom Vroom!
PATTERNS

The Best Bug Parade
COMPARING SIZES

Double the Ducks
DOUBLING NUMBERS

The Greatest Gymnast of All
OPPOSITES

A House for Birdie
UNDERSTANDING CAPACITY

It's About Time!
HOURS

Jack the Builder
COUNTING ON

Leaping Lizards
COUNTING BY 5s AND 10s

Mighty Maddie
COMPARING WEIGHTS

Missing Mittens
ODD AND EVEN NUMBERS

Monster Musical Chairs
SUBTRACTING ONE

One...Two...Three...Sassafras!
NUMBER ORDER

A Pair of Socks
MATCHING

3 Little Fire Fighters
SORTING

LEVEL 2

Bigger, Better, Best!
AREA

Coyotes All Around
ROUNDING

Get Up and Go!
TIME LINES

Give Me Half!
UNDERSTANDING HALVES

Mall Mania
ADDITION STRATEGIES

More or Less
COMPARING NUMBERS

100 Days of Cool
NUMBERS 1-100

Pepper's Journal
CALENDARS

Probably Pistachio
PROBABILITY

Same Old Horse
MAKING PREDICTIONS

Spunky Monkeys on Parade
COUNTING BY 2s, 3s, AND 4s

The Sundae Scoop
COMBINATIONS

Super Sand Castle Saturday
MEASURING

Tally O'Malley
TALLYING

LEVEL 3

Betcha!
ESTIMATING

Dinosaur Deals
EQUIVALENT VALUES

Divide and Ride
DIVIDING

Earth Day—Hooray!
PLACE VALUE

The Grizzly Gazette
PERCENTAGE

Hamster Champs
ANGLES

Lemonade for Sale
BAR GRAPHS

Less Than Zero
NEGATIVE NUMBERS

Polly's Pen Pal
METRICS

Rodeo Time
READING A SCHEDULE

Safari Park
FINDING UNKNOWNS

Shark Swimathon
SUBTRACTING TWO-DIGIT NUMBERS

Sluggers' Car Wash
DOLLARS AND CENTS

Treasure Map
MAPPING

Katie and Cameron couldn't wait for the rodeo to start. This year they weren't just going to watch. They were going to do all sorts of jobs for their uncle, Cactus Joe, the best bull rider in Texas.

The night before the rodeo began, Cactus Joe came by to tell them about their first chore—to water the horses before the Bareback Bronc Riding event.

"It starts at 3:00, so be there at 2:00 sharp," he said. "You'll need an hour to get the job done."

Katie made a schedule so they'd be sure to be on time.

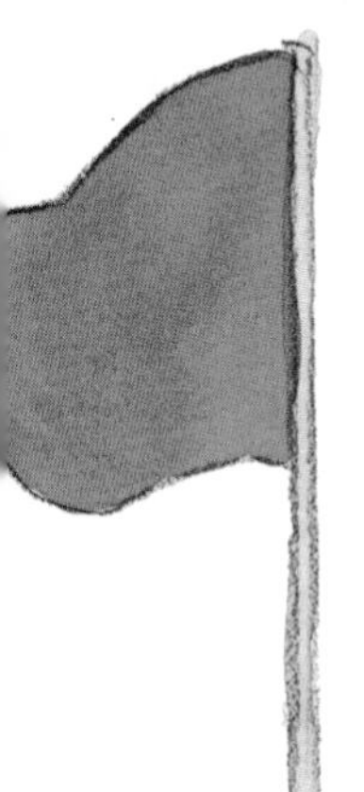

Katie and Cameron loved the Parade and the Grand Entry. They were the last to leave the stands.

"We'd better get lunch quickly so we can make it to our job on time," said Katie.

“I want a burrito,” Cameron said. “No, barbecue. No, chili. No . . .”

Cameron changed his mind at every stand. Katie had finished her taco before her brother finally bought a chicken-fried steak sandwich.

Just after Cameron took his first bite, Katie looked at her watch.

"Oh no!" she yelled. "It's way past 2:00! We've got to go!"

When Katie and Cameron got to the holding pen, there was Cactus Joe. "Sorry, cowpokes," he said. "You were late, so I watered the horses myself."

Katie and Cameron felt terrible. They climbed into the stands for the Bareback Bronc Riding.

"We have to do better tomorrow," Katie said.

That night, after the Campfire Sing-Along, Cactus Joe asked, "Want to try again?" He then gave them a job for the following day—catching the calves that got loose on their way to the Calf Roping, which started at 3:00. "You'll have to be there by 2:30, pronto," he said.

Cameron made another schedule.

Katie and Cameron cheered for the barrel racers. They both got chili for lunch. But at the Livestock Show, Cameron stopped to look at the prize-winning chickens, and Katie lingered at a pen full of lambs.

Then Cameron looked at his watch.
"Oh no!" he said. "We've only got 10 minutes!"

"Just on time!" said Cactus Joe as Katie and Cameron ran up.
All the calves were herded out of the barn and toward the arena.

"Good work!" said Cactus Joe. "I guess you're ready for a really important job tomorrow."

That night, after the Fiddling Contest, Cactus Joe told them about their biggest job yet—handing out the ribbons for the Bull Riding Championship, Cactus Joe's special event.

"You'll have to be at the grandstand at exactly 4:45," he said. "Why don't you put the end time of each event in your schedule so you'll be sure to make it?"

Katie and Cameron cheered for the bull ropers, ate as much barbecue as they could hold, and whooped for the saddle bronc riders. But they kept a careful eye on the time.

A little before 4:15, Katie said, "Let's leave early so we have plenty of time to get to the grandstand."

But then a bunch of clowns came by on bicycles.

"Excuse us—we need to get through!" said Katie. But no one could hear her.

Then came the sheep.

"Hey, watch out!" said Cameron.

"Hurry up!" yelled Katie.

They started to run. But Cameron didn't see the blue-ribbon pig.

Katie landed right on top of Cameron.

"Now we'll never make it!" he wailed.

"What's wrong?" asked one of the clowns, sweeping up on his bicycle.

Katie explained. "We'll be late," she said sadly, "and we tried so hard to be on time."

"You won't be late," said the clown. "Climb on!"

And Katie and Cameron sped off toward the arena on the back of the clown's bicycle.

"Yeeeee-ha!" shouted Cameron.

They made it just in time to watch the bull riding up close.

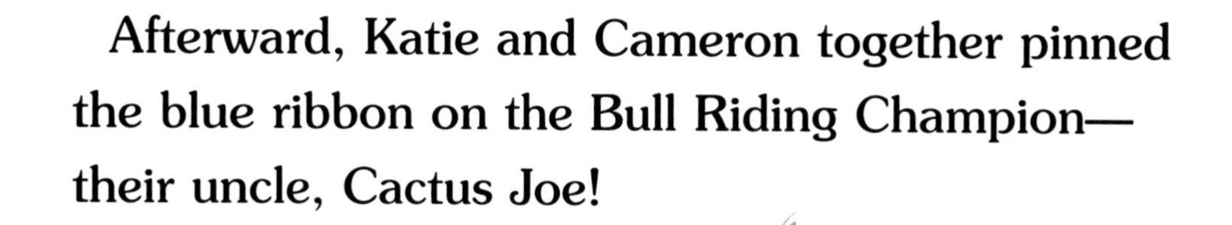

Afterward, Katie and Cameron together pinned the blue ribbon on the Bull Riding Champion—their uncle, Cactus Joe!

FOR ADULTS AND KIDS

In *Rodeo Time*, the math concept is reading a schedule. Understanding a schedule involves time-telling skills such as being able to read the hours, half hours, and minutes on a clock; having a sense of elapsed time; and planning well.

If you would like to have more fun with the math concepts presented in *Rodeo Time*, here are a few suggestions:

- As you read the story together, refer back to the schedule that Katie and Cameron made for each day and compare the schedule to the times shown in the illustrations.

- Ask questions throughout the story, such as "How much time is there between the parade and lunch?" and "If the clock says 4:15, how much time is there before the children need to be in the grandstand?"

- After reading the story, help the child make a time schedule of a typical day in his or her school. Discuss how long each activity takes. What is the child's favorite time of the day?

- Together, make a schedule of what the child is planning to do the next day. Later, have the child record what he or she actually did. Compare the record of the day to the schedule.

- Talk about occupations that use time schedules. For example, doctors, dentists, coaches, and teachers all use schedules to plan their days. Make a schedule for your workday and review it with the child.

Following are some activities that will help you extend the concepts presented in *Rodeo Time* into a child's everyday life:

Making Plans: Plan a visit to an amusement park or a fair. Make a time schedule of what you would like to see and do.

Watching TV: On index cards, write the names and times of TV programs the family views on any given day. Mix the cards up and have the child put them in order from earliest to latest. Then figure out how long each program airs. How much time is there between programs?

Estimating Time: Have the child write down the beginning time of an activity, such as taking a bath or doing homework, and estimate how much time it will take. When he or she is finished, check the actual time to see how close the estimate was. Repeat with other activities.

The following books include some of the same concepts that are presented in *Rodeo Time*:

- THE SUN'S DAY by Mordicai Gerstein
- PIGS ON A BLANKET by Amy Axelrod
- WHAT TIME IS IT, MR. CROCODILE? by Judy Sierra